Fostering Empowering Habits

Activating Your Potential and Charting a Course to Success

Camilla Brooke

Disclaimer

Table of Contents

Introduction

In the vast landscape of personal and professional growth lies a terrain marked by the indelible imprints of success—a destination coveted by many yet achieved by a select few. "Indispensable Habits for Success" beckons readers into the realm of transformation, offering not just a glimpse but an immersive journey into the core principles that separate the extraordinary from the ordinary.

As we traverse through the pages of this compelling exploration, the veil is lifted on the elusive secrets that underpin lasting success. No mere compilation of clichéd advice, this book is a blueprint for the relentless pursuit of greatness, weaving together the threads of wisdom, discipline, and resilience. It's an invitation to challenge the status quo and forge a path that leads not only to achievement but to a profound sense of fulfillment.

The canvas painted by these indispensable habits is not confined to the professional sphere alone; it extends into the very fabric of one's being. Rooted in the understanding that success is an intricate tapestry of thought, action, and character, each habit encapsulates a transformative principle that, when woven together, creates a masterpiece of achievement. This isn't just a manual for success; it's a manifesto for a life well lived.

Prepare to be captivated by the narratives of individuals who have walked this path and emerged not just victorious but as architects of their own destiny. "Indispensable Habits for Success" is not merely a book; it is an odyssey, a guide, and a catalyst for those who dare to dream beyond the ordinary and aspire to carve their legacy in the annals of success. Welcome to a journey where each page is a step closer to unlocking the extraordinary within you.

Chapter 1

Cultivating a Proactive Mindset

In the vast tapestry of success, the first brushstroke is the proactive mindset—a foundational hue that sets the tone for the masterpiece of achievement. It's not merely a state of mind but a dynamic force that propels individuals beyond the realm of reaction into the realm of intentional creation.

A proactive mindset begins with the recognition that we are the architects of our own destinies. It is a conscious choice to seize control of our thoughts, actions, and responses to external stimuli. In understanding that circumstances do not dictate our outcomes, but rather our responses to those circumstances, we unveil the true power of proactivity.

This chapter unravels the intricacies of cultivating a Proactive Mindset, providing practical insights and actionable strategies. It delves into the art of taking initiative, empowering readers to break free from the shackles of passivity and chart their course with purpose. It explores the concept of responsibility, urging individuals to embrace accountability for their choices and outcomes.

Through real-life examples and thought-provoking exercises, readers are invited to assess their current mindset and envision the transformative potential of a proactive approach. The proactive mindset is not a one-size-fits-all formula; it's a personalized journey of self-discovery and empowerment.

Moreso, in the symphony of personal development, the proactive mindset serves as the conductor, orchestrating the harmonious melodies of intentional living. This chapter invites you to delve deep into the essence of proactivity—an art form that transcends mere reactions to external stimuli, transforming them into purposeful actions.

At its core, a Proactive Mindset propels us beyond the confines of circumstance. It's a conscious decision to wield the brush and paint our life's canvas with bold strokes of choice and responsibility. This chapter illuminates the notion that we are not passive spectators in the theater of life; instead, we are active participants capable of shaping our narratives.

Journeying through the pages, we unravel the intricacies of taking initiative—the spark that ignites the flame of proactive living. Through compelling stories and practical exercises, you'll witness how individuals turned adversity into opportunity by embracing a proactive stance. It's about navigating life's challenges not as obstacles but as stepping stones toward personal and professional triumph.

Responsibility becomes our compass in this exploration, guiding us through the labyrinth of choices. We explore the liberating power of acknowledging our agency, understanding that every decision carries the potential to sculpt our destiny. By assuming accountability for our actions, we step into the realm of empowerment, where challenges become catalysts for growth.

This chapter isn't just a discourse on theory; it's a call to action. As you engage with the material, consider this not as a passive reading but as a dynamic workshop for self-discovery. Together, let us peel away the layers of reactive thinking and embrace the transformative force of a Proactive Mindset. The journey unfolds, and the possibilities are limitless—are you ready to seize them? Let the exploration commence.

Chapter 2

Envisioning Success: Begin with the End in Mind

In the grand tapestry of achievement, the second chapter beckons us to embark on a profound journey—one that starts with a clear vision of the destination. "Begin with the End in Mind" is not merely a roadmap; it's a compass guiding us through the complexities of goal-setting, vision crafting, and the deliberate cultivation of a future-oriented perspective.

This chapter serves as a beacon, illuminating the transformative power of envisioning success before it becomes a tangible reality. It challenges us to transcend the immediate and glimpse into the horizon of our aspirations, where each step is purposefully aligned with the overarching narrative of our lives.

We explore the art of setting goals that transcend the ordinary—goals that resonate with our deepest values and aspirations. Through introspective exercises and illustrative anecdotes, we navigate the intricacies of crafting a personal vision statement, a compass that keeps us on course amid life's myriad distractions.

"Begin with the End in Mind" is not about predicting the future but about actively participating in its creation. It's a call to architect our destinies with intention, to dream not only for the sake of dreaming but as a prelude to a deliberate and purposeful reality.

As we journey through this chapter, let us challenge ourselves to embrace the transformative potential of forward-thinking. This is not just a chapter on goal-setting; it's an invitation to become architects of our fate, designing a future that resonates with our deepest desires. Are you ready to shape your destiny from the vantage point of your dreams? The odyssey begins here.

Chapter 3

Prioritizing Purpose: Put First Things First

In the intricate dance of productivity and purpose, the third chapter beckons us to explore the art of intentional living— a realm where priorities align seamlessly with our deepest values. "Put First Things First" transcends the mere act of time management; it is a symphony of choices that resonate with the melody of our most significant aspirations.

This chapter is a compass, guiding us through the labyrinth of daily decisions and commitments. It's a call to examine not just how we spend our time, but why we allocate it to particular pursuits. Through a lens of purposeful prioritization, we navigate the delicate balance between the urgent and the important, ensuring that our actions align with our overarching goals.

We delve into practical strategies for effective time management, understanding that it is not about doing more but doing what truly matters. The concept of the time matrix becomes our ally, empowering us to distinguish between tasks that contribute to our long-term vision and those that merely demand immediate attention.

"Put First Things First" is a mantra for those seeking not only productivity but fulfillment. It challenges us to embrace a paradigm shift—a mindset where we cultivate the courage to say no to the trivial to make room for the significant. Through real-life anecdotes and actionable insights, this chapter is an invitation to reclaim control over our time and, by extension, our destiny.

As we navigate this chapter, let us unravel the threads of purpose woven into our daily choices. This is not merely a discourse on time management; it's a transformative exploration of living in alignment with our deepest values. Are you ready to prioritize purpose and put first things first? The journey awaits.

Chapter 4

Collaboration and Abundance: Think Win-Win

In the intricate dance of interpersonal dynamics and shared aspirations, the fourth chapter extends an invitation to embrace a paradigm of mutual success — "Think Win-Win." This chapter transcends conventional notions of competition and rivalry; it's a philosophy that heralds collaboration and abundance as keystones to lasting success.

"Think Win-Win" is not merely a negotiation tactic but a mindset that fosters a belief in shared victories. It challenges the notion that success is a zero-sum game and, instead, invites us to explore the vast landscape of cooperative possibilities where everyone involved can emerge triumphant.

This chapter serves as a guide, navigating us through the nuances of collaborative thinking and the power of synergistic partnerships.

Through engaging narratives and practical strategies, it unfolds the transformative potential of seeking solutions where all parties involved benefit—where success is not exclusive but inclusive.

We delve into the art of effective communication, recognizing that fostering a "Think Win-Win" mentality requires not only expressing our needs but also empathetically understanding the needs of others. This is a shift from a scarcity mindset to one of abundance, where success is seen as limitless and attainable for all.

As we traverse this chapter, let us challenge ourselves to transcend the traditional win-lose mentality and embrace a perspective that cultivates flourishing connections and shared triumphs. "Think Win-Win" is more than a chapter; it's an exploration of a mindset that transforms not only our interactions but the very fabric of our success. Are you ready to forge alliances that elevate everyone involved? The journey into collaborative abundance begins here.

Chapter 5

Sympathetic Correspondence - Look for First to Comprehend, Then to Be Perceived

In the intricate dance of human connection and effective communication, the fifth chapter extends an invitation to delve into the profound art of empathy: "Look for First to Comprehend, Then to Be Perceived." This part rises above the shallow layers of discourse; It takes a comprehensive look at the transformative power of listening and comprehension as the fundamental components of effective communication.

"Seek First to Understand, Then to Be Understood" is not just a communication strategy but a philosophy that challenges us to prioritize understanding others before asserting our own perspectives. It's a recognition that true communication is a two-way street, where the exchange of ideas is enriched by a genuine and empathetic comprehension of the other person's viewpoint.

This chapter serves as a guide, leading us through the intricacies of active listening and the cultivation of empathy. Through illustrative stories and practical exercises, it unveils the profound impact of approaching conversations with a genuine desire to comprehend the thoughts, feelings, and perspectives of others.

We delve into the nuances of effective communication, recognizing that empathy is the bridge that connects diverse perspectives and fosters deeper connections. This is not merely about expressing ourselves; it's about creating a space where every voice is heard and understood.

As we navigate this chapter, let us challenge ourselves to transcend the noise of everyday communication and embrace the transformative power of seeking first to understand. This is more than a chapter; it's an exploration of empathy as a catalyst for profound connections and a cornerstone for success. Are you ready to communicate not just with words but with understanding? The journey into empathetic communication begins here.

Chapter 6

Fostering Collective Brilliance: Synergize

In the intricate dance of collective endeavors, the sixth chapter extends an enticing invitation to explore the transformative symphony of synergy—a harmonious collaboration where individual talents, ideas, and energies converge to produce results that transcend the capabilities of each contributor. "Synergize" is not merely a call for teamwork; it's an exploration of the alchemy that transpires when diverse minds come together with a shared purpose, creating a collective brilliance greater than the sum of its parts.

As our guide through this chapter, we embark on a journey that navigates the art of synergistic collaboration. It's a compass pointing towards a realm where the whole becomes more than the mere aggregation of its components. Through captivating narratives and actionable insights, we unravel the layers of collaborative brilliance, emphasizing the strength found in embracing diverse perspectives and capitalizing on the unique strengths each team member brings to the collective canvas.

Effective teamwork, as illuminated in "Synergize," is not a homogeneous endeavor but a celebration of differences. It challenges the notion that success is an individual pursuit, inviting us to recognize that true innovation and breakthroughs arise when individuals unite, each contributing their distinct abilities to a shared vision. The chapter goes beyond the mechanics of collaboration; it is a revelation of the profound impact when synergy becomes a guiding principle, sparking creativity and fostering an environment where collective brilliance thrives.

In navigating this chapter, the reader is encouraged to challenge preconceived notions of solitary success and embrace the extraordinary possibilities that unfold when collaboration becomes an art form. "Synergize" is not a mere instructional guide; it is an exploration of the vibrant tapestry that emerges when diverse talents come together to synergize for a common purpose. Are you prepared to witness the transformative alchemy that occurs when individuals unite in a symphony of creativity? The journey into fostering collective brilliance unfolds here, inviting you to witness the magic that happens when collaboration becomes more than a strategy—it becomes an ethos.

Chapter 7

Nurturing Wholeness: Sharpen the Saw

In the rhythm of life's demands and personal growth, the seventh chapter extends a gentle yet powerful invitation to reflect on the profound principle of "Sharpen the Saw." Beyond the hustle and bustle of daily tasks, this chapter beckons us to prioritize self-renewal and well-being as essential components of sustained effectiveness.

As the guiding force through this exploration, the chapter unfolds as a compass, navigating us through the dimensions of physical, mental, emotional, and spiritual well-being. It is an acknowledgment that, like a saw dulled by continuous use, our capacities can diminish without intentional renewal. Through compelling anecdotes and practical strategies, the chapter unveils the importance of regularly honing these facets to maintain a state of optimal balance.

Physical rejuvenation, as emphasized in "Sharpen the Saw," transcends conventional notions of exercise. It encompasses nourishing the body through healthy nutrition, adequate rest, and regular physical activity. This section challenges us to view our bodies not merely as instruments but as temples that require deliberate care for sustained vitality.

Mental stimulation is another facet explored in the chapter. It delves into the significance of continuous learning and mental exercises to enhance cognitive abilities. From acquiring new skills to engaging in activities that challenge the mind, the chapter underscores the idea that mental sharpness is a lifelong pursuit that contributes significantly to personal and professional effectiveness.

The emotional dimension of well-being is not overlooked. The chapter discusses the importance of fostering positive relationships, practicing empathy, and managing stress. It encourages readers to understand and express their emotions effectively, recognizing that emotional well-being is intricately connected to overall life satisfaction.

Lastly, the spiritual aspect of "Sharpen the Saw" invites contemplation and connection with one's core values. It explores practices that bring a sense of purpose and meaning, reminding us that personal growth is a holistic journey encompassing the alignment of our actions with our deepest beliefs.

In navigating this chapter, readers are urged to consider the metaphorical saws they wield in their lives—their bodies, minds, emotions, and spirits—and to recognize the transformative power that intentional self-renewal holds. "Sharpen the Saw" is not just a chapter; it's an invitation to cultivate a life of wholeness, where personal well-being becomes the foundation for sustained effectiveness. Are you ready to embark on the journey of self-renewal and experience the transformative impact it can have on your life? The odyssey begins here.

Chapter 8

Unleashing Peak Efficiency: 30 Habits Practiced by High Achievers for Enhanced Productivity

1. They enjoy continuous reprieves to re-establish energy.

2. They're driven by purpose.

3. They create their to-do list the night before (and break major tasks into sub-tasks).

4. They prevent internal distractions.

5. They keep a separate to-do list for external distractions.

6. They optimize their email with smart tools.

7. They incorporate sound propensities into their everyday daily practice.

8. They are lightning quick on the PC.

9. They have a "growth mindset."

10. They outsource mindless tasks.

11. They meditate.

12. They say no (nicely).

13. They count their blessings.

14. They avoid decision fatigue.

15. They love productivity hacks.

16. They Cultivate a Positive and Resilient Mindset

17. They Cultivate a Learning Mindset

18. They Practice Effective Decision Making

19. They Collaborate and Delegate

20. They Embrace Continuous Improvement

21. They Embrace a Growth Mindset

22. They Practice Mindfulness and Meditation

23. They Maintain a Clutter-Free Workspace

24. They Seek Feedback and Learn from Others

25. They Automate and Streamline Processes

26. They Practice Effective Goal Tracking

27. They Embrace a Balanced Lifestyle

28. They Foster a Supportive Network

29. They Continuously Learn and Adapt

30. They Celebrate Achievements

Whether in your professional or personal life, implementing these habits will empower you to make the most of your time, energy, and resources, ultimately unlocking your full potential and achieving your goals.

So, embrace these habits, stay consistent, and prepare to achieve greatness.

Conclusion

As we draw the final curtain on our exploration of the habits that propel individuals toward heightened productivity, let us reflect on the transformative journey we've undertaken together. In these pages, we have navigated the intricate pathways of proactive thinking, visionary goal-setting, prioritized action, collaborative mindset, empathetic communication, synergistic collaboration, and holistic self-renewal.

Productivity, we've discovered, is not merely a result of efficient task management but a reflection of the habits and mindset that shape our daily endeavors. It is a symphony of intentional choices, continuous learning, and a commitment to both personal and collective growth.

As you close this book, consider this not just a manual on productivity but a companion in your ongoing quest for excellence. The habits we've explored are not a rigid formula but a flexible framework, inviting you to adapt and integrate them into your unique journey.

May these insights linger in your thoughts as gentle reminders, nudging you towards a proactive mindset when challenges arise, urging you to envision success before taking the first step, guiding you to prioritize purpose in your daily actions, encouraging collaboration and understanding in your interactions, fostering synergy in your collective efforts, and emphasizing the importance of self-renewal in sustaining your journey.

In the grand tapestry of life, productivity becomes a reflection of our commitment to growth, contribution, and the pursuit of meaningful accomplishments. As you step forward, may these habits be the silent companions that accompany you on your path to success. Remember, it's not just about what you achieve but also how you become, and in cultivating these habits, you sculpt a version of yourself capable of extraordinary accomplishments.

May your endeavors be purposeful, your collaborations fruitful, and your journey towards productivity and fulfillment be a source of continuous inspiration. Here's to the habits that transform routine into mastery and to the journey that unfolds beyond the pages of this book—a journey marked by a sustained commitment to becoming the most productive and fulfilled version of yourself.

www.ingramcontent.com/pod-product-compliance
Lightning Source LLC
Chambersburg PA
CBHW072331270726
48658CB00016B/2293